OK, BOOMER

OK, BOOMER

USING A LANDLINE, GOING TO THE POST OFFICE, and other OUTDATED THINGS YOU DON'T NEED ANYMORE

TILLER PRESS
New York London Toronto Sydney New Delhi

An Imprint of Simon & Schuster, Inc.
1230 Avenue of the Americas
New York, NY 10020

First Tiller Press hardcover edition October 2020

Interior design by Jennifer Chung

Illustrations by Ashlee Beadle

Manufactured in the United States of America

1 3 5 7 9 10 8 6 4 2

Library of Congress Control Number: 2020931544

ISBN 978-1-9821-5459-2
ISBN 978-1-9821-5460-8 (ebook)

To Boomers everywhere

Introduction

Leaving voice mails.

Owning a VCR.

Insisting that the GPS must be wrong.

Expressing skepticism about global warming.

There are dozens of outdated errands, items, and beliefs that Baby Boomers just can't seem to give up. No matter how many times Millennials and Gen Zers attempt to drag them into 2020, Boomers simply stamp their feet and insist that they must arrive at the airport seven hours early.

So if, after failing once again to explain why no one uses an encyclopedia anymore, you've thrown your hands up and screamed, "OK, Boomer!" then this book is for you. Containing fifty-eight classic Boomerisms that you can laugh, sigh, or roll your eyes at, *OK, Boomer* is the perfect vent for your rage at receiving another crazy conspiracy theory from a Yahoo e-mail address.

Look at that snow outside. We could really use some global warming right now.

OK, BOOMER.

Our flight leaves in
seven hours.
We should head to
the airport now!

OK, BOOMER.

Jell-O salads are perfect for any party!

OK, BOOMER.

When I graduated from college, I just walked right into the company where I wanted to work and asked for a job!

OK, BOOMER.

Call the landline.

OK, BOOMER.

I saw it on *Law & Order*.

OK, BOOMER.

Salads are rabbit food.

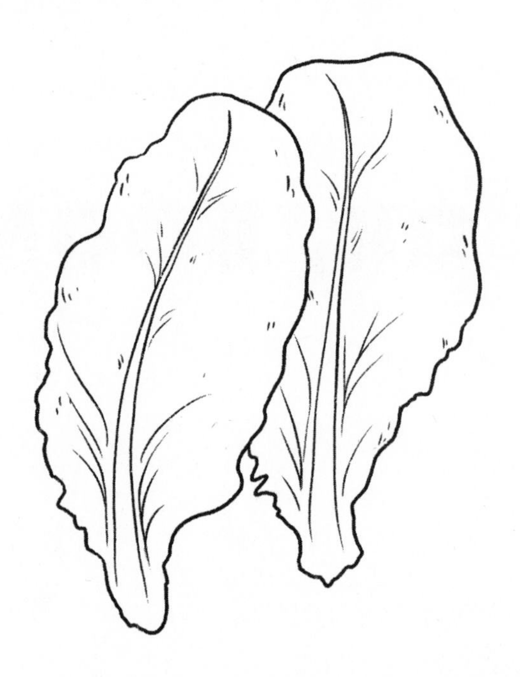

OK, BOOMER.

I bought it from the
Home Shopping Network.

OK, BOOMER.

Why did they get rid of the killer whales at SeaWorld? Shamu was great!

OK, BOOMER.

My email address is
*******@yahoo.com.**

OK, BOOMER.

I taped it on VHS.

OK, BOOMER.

The Wi-Fi password is
35309752474342594305.

OK, BOOMER.

Did you see my Facebook post?

OK, BOOMER.

I don't need a GPS.

OK, BOOMER.

How the heck do you
turn this thing on?

OK, BOOMER.

Maybe you could try dropping off your résumé in person.

OK, BOOMER.

I read the newspaper today, and there was a front-page article on . . .

OK, BOOMER.

I heard Alex Jones say it.

OK, BOOMER.

Why take the bus or the train? It's easier to drive.

OK, BOOMER.

Let’s go to
Olive Garden.

OK, BOOMER.

Did you get my
voice mail?

OK, BOOMER.

Let me write a check for that.

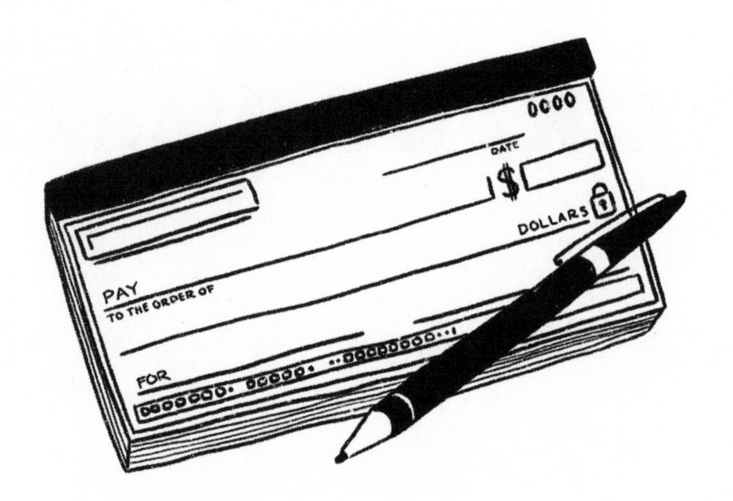

OK, BOOMER.

You can't find a job on the Internet. You need to go out and pound the pavement.

OK, BOOMER.

Fuzzy toilet-seat covers.

OK, BOOMER.

[Talking to Google Home]
"Siri?"

OK, BOOMER.

I printed out the directions from MapQuest.

OK, BOOMER.

Let's go on a cruise!

OK, BOOMER.

I need to go to the bank.

OK, BOOMER.

Margarine.

OK, BOOMER.

Socks with sandals are sensible fashion.

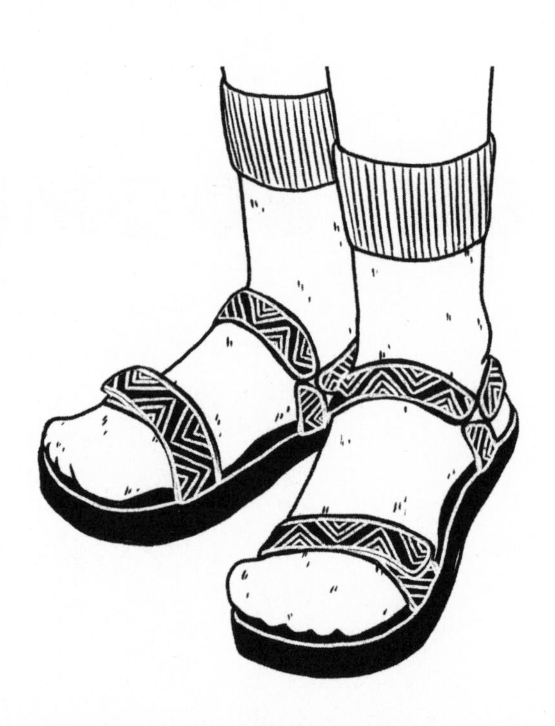

OK, BOOMER.

Let’s go to the mall!

OK, BOOMER.

Time to watch
***Wheel of Fortune*!**

OK, BOOMER.

Look up the number in the phone book.

OK, BOOMER.

Make sure you iron it before you wear it.

OK, BOOMER.

I read it in
***Reader's Digest*.**

OK, BOOMER.

Watching golf on TV.

OK, BOOMER.

Are you keeping your checkbook balanced?

OK, BOOMER.

I need to go to the post office.

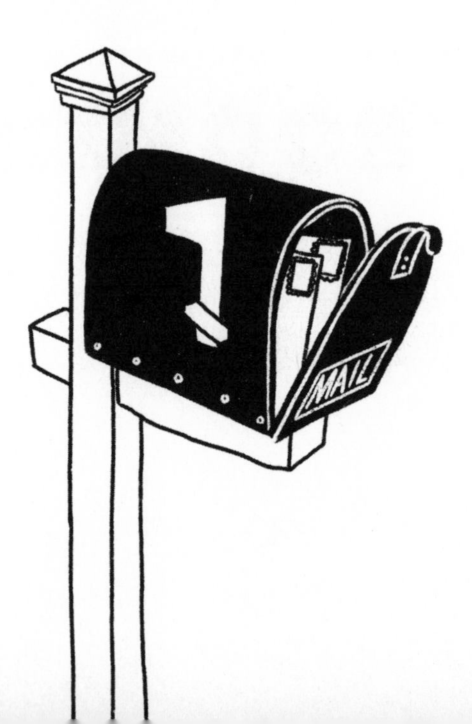

OK, BOOMER.

Anything will taste better with some Mrs. Dash.

OK, BOOMER.

Meat loaf.

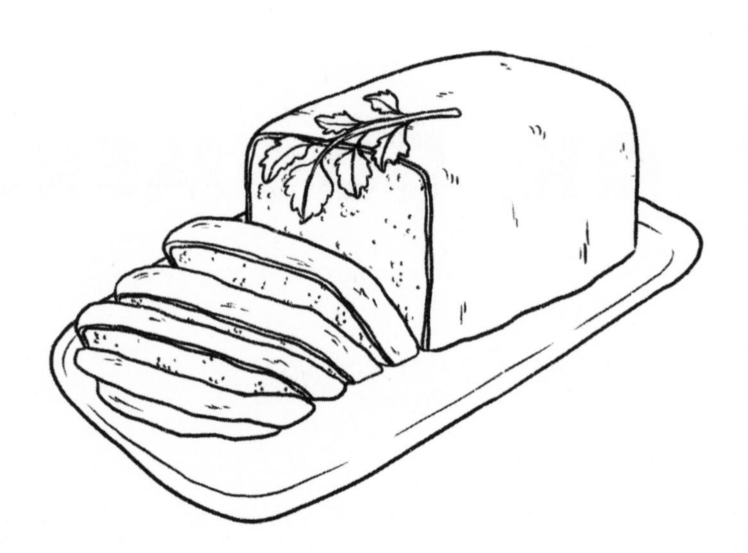

OK, BOOMER.

SENDING E-MAILS IN ALL CAPS, BECAUSE THAT DEFINITELY GETS THE POINT ACROSS.

ok, boomer.

Bar soap.

OK, BOOMER.

I just put up some
nice patterned wallpaper
in my bathroom.

OK, BOOMER.

Doing sudoku in pen.

OK, BOOMER.

I pay all my bills by mail.

OK, BOOMER.

Raquetball.

OK, BOOMER.

Did you hear the latest about [insert random conspiracy theory here]?

OK, BOOMER.

One can never have too many throw pillows.

OK, BOOMER.

[Making your ringtone
as loud as possible.]

OK, BOOMER.

I bought it from a mail-order catalog that I subscribe to.

OK, BOOMER.

Have you read the new Danielle Steel novel?

OK, BOOMER.

I should check the answering machine.

OK, BOOMER.

[After buying anything]
What's the damage?

OK, BOOMER.

Saying “oof”
when sitting down.

OK, BOOMER.

Look it up in the encyclopedia.

OK, BOOMER.

Let's watch *Dateline*.

OK, BOOMER.

[Shouting at the
automated customer-
service system]
Operator! Representative!
Customer-service agent!
Human! Anyone!

OK, BOOMER.

Millennials are entitled and selfish.

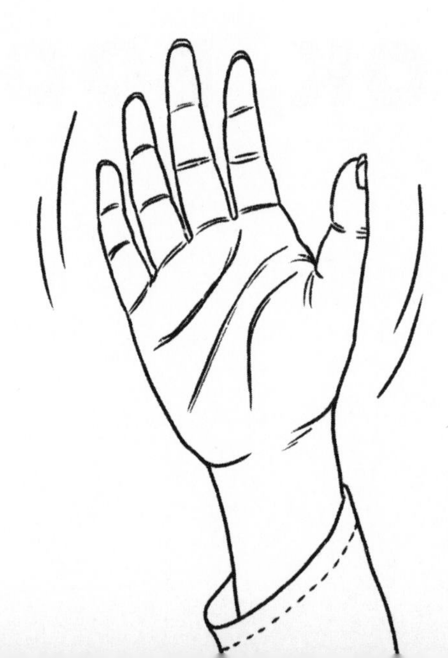

OK, BOOMER.